N A

I basically did the
whole thing.

X E D

You are here

4

6

12

74

118

PROLOGUE

I used to hate haiku. I couldn't see beauty in poetry that didn't rhyme for I thought the "limitation" of the rhyme, the fact that there are less words for you to use to say what you are trying to say, was what made poetry beautiful, and that's why I had never been interested in haiku until I wrote one. That's when I understood the beauty of haiku also laid on the limitation, in this case, the limitation of the number of syllables you have at hand and that force you to find the essence of what you are trying to say because with 17 syllables, there is no room for floursishings, you have to make every syllable count.

As contradictory as it may sound, the following poems weren't written as a mean to entertain, they've been my therapy for the past year and a half of battling depression, anxiety, and lately, many suicidal and self-desctructive thoughts. Most of them came from the inner necessity to vent so I was never forcing myself to write them, they were always written out of need.

As someone who tends to keep things to myself, I've never wanted to bother a third party with my problems, instead, these provide a creative way for me to deal with my mental health, for I can try to create something beautiful (or at least, that was the intention, despite the cryptic and depressive nature of the some of the poems) out of something dark rather than trying to bury or ignore all these thoughts and voices in my head.

I would also like to apologize to the reader for I'm aware that the nature of some of these poems is quite dark and I am, in no way, trying to romanticize depression, I'm just trying to deal with it in the best way that I can.

A Haiku is a

poem that has five, seven,

and five syllables.

naked

勿体

勿体無い・ **Mottainai**

1. (adj-i) impious; profane; sacrilegious
2. too good; more than one deserves; unworthy of
3. wasteful

CHAPTER 1

無い

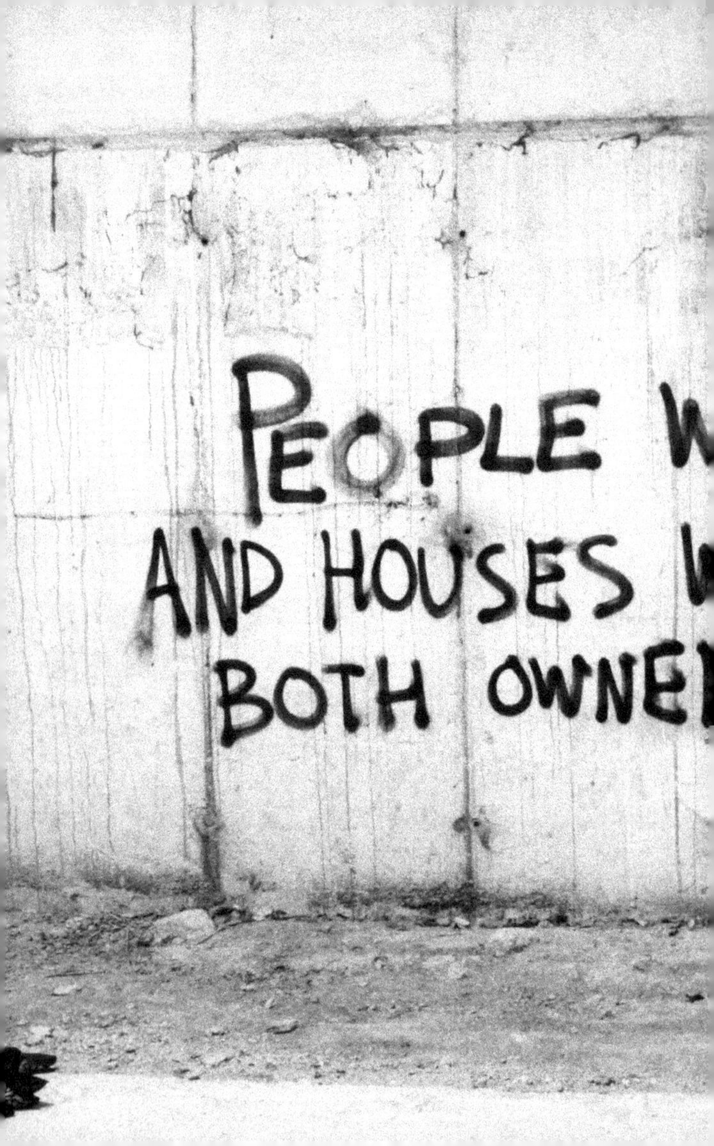

PEOPLE W
AND HOUSES W
BOTH OWNE

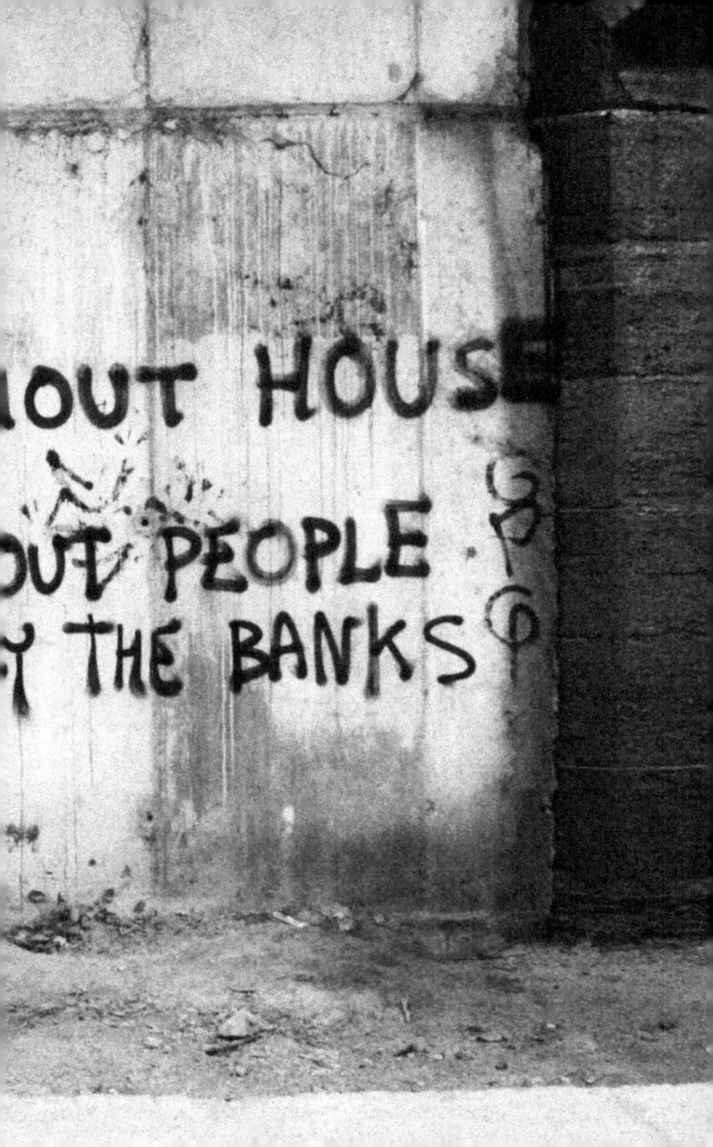

OUT HOUSE
OUT PEOPLE
THE BANKS

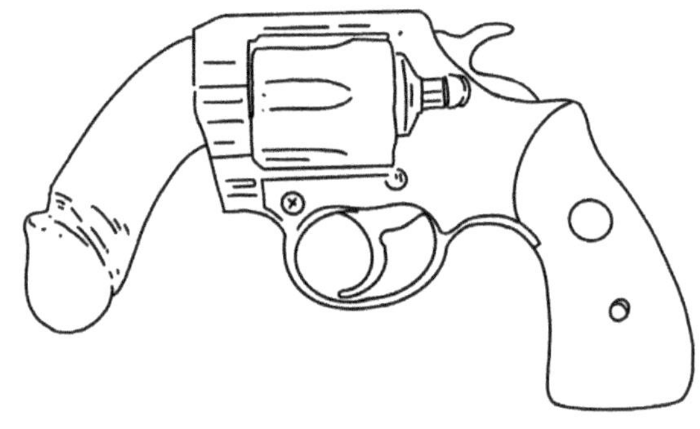

Guns do not protect,
they fill the voids in the pants
of men with small dicks.

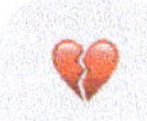

It is depressing
and never like the movies.
It kills you inside.

Wonder what you did
to achieve whiteness 'fore you
hate those with dark skin.

hate those with dark skin.
to achieve whiteness 'fore you
Wonder what you did

YOUR GRIEF IS MY HELL,
MY COLOR THE RULING THAT
CONDONES THE TORTURES.

LiES WILL KEEP

iGNORANCE WILL

i ENVY

THEM SANE

KEEP THEM BLIND

THEM FOOLS

*Oh, to hold your hand
while watching the world collapse
and burn to ashes.*

Just a pond of noise
in an ocean of silence
with drops of music.

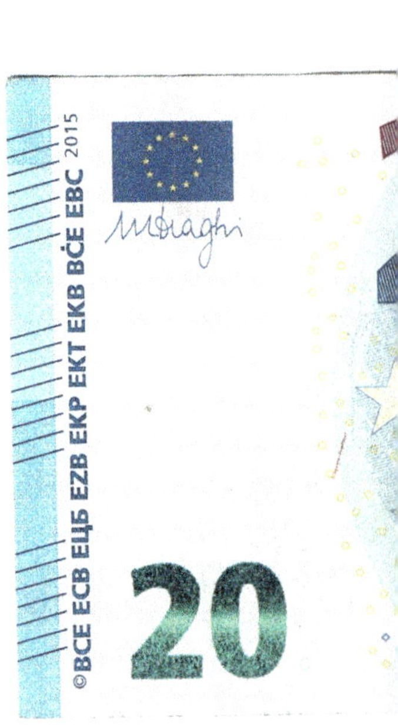

My aunt: I hate her.
She is a fucking psycho
(In medical terms).

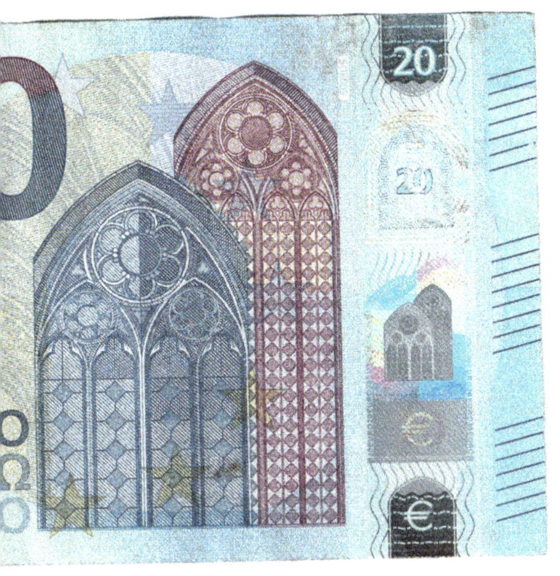

Stones that ease the pain,
crystals that cure brain cancer:
Frauds that make them rich.

That weightless feeling,
reminiscent of the womb.
Pure silence and peace.

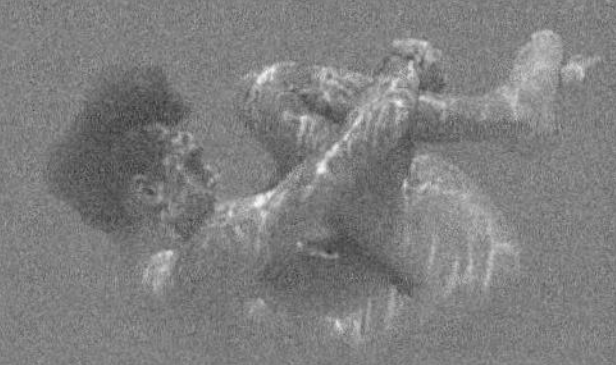

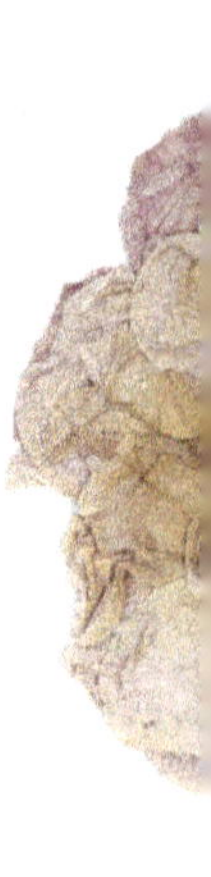

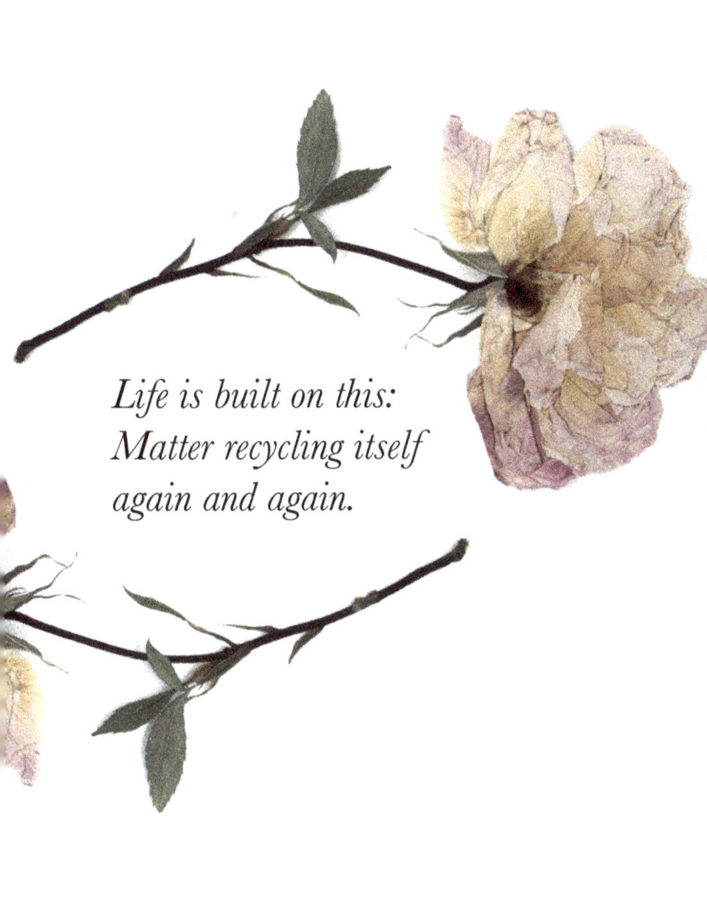

Life is built on this:
Matter recycling itself
again and again.

*Thick layers of sand
covering ancient temples.
No god survives time.*

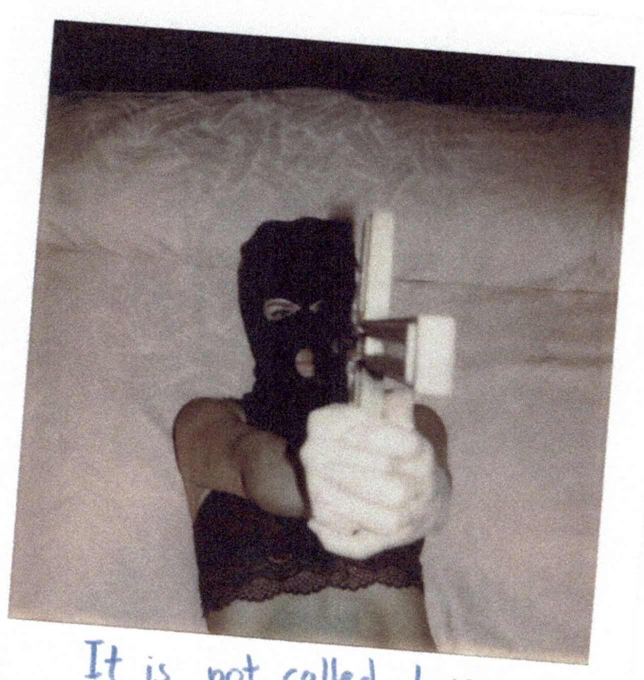

It is not called love,
if they threaten you with hell
It's called "blackmailing"

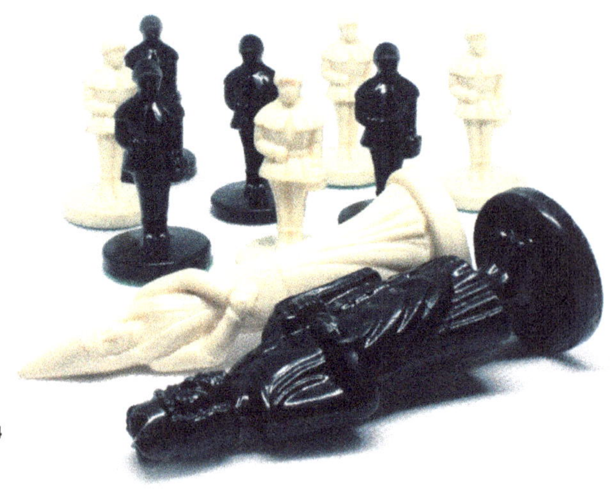

44

*Kings live off the sweat
of those who work, dreaming of
things they can't attain.*

*Empty my head, till
it's all stars and stripes, send me
to a certain death.*

*The last thing I need
to remember you raped me
is your bastard son.*

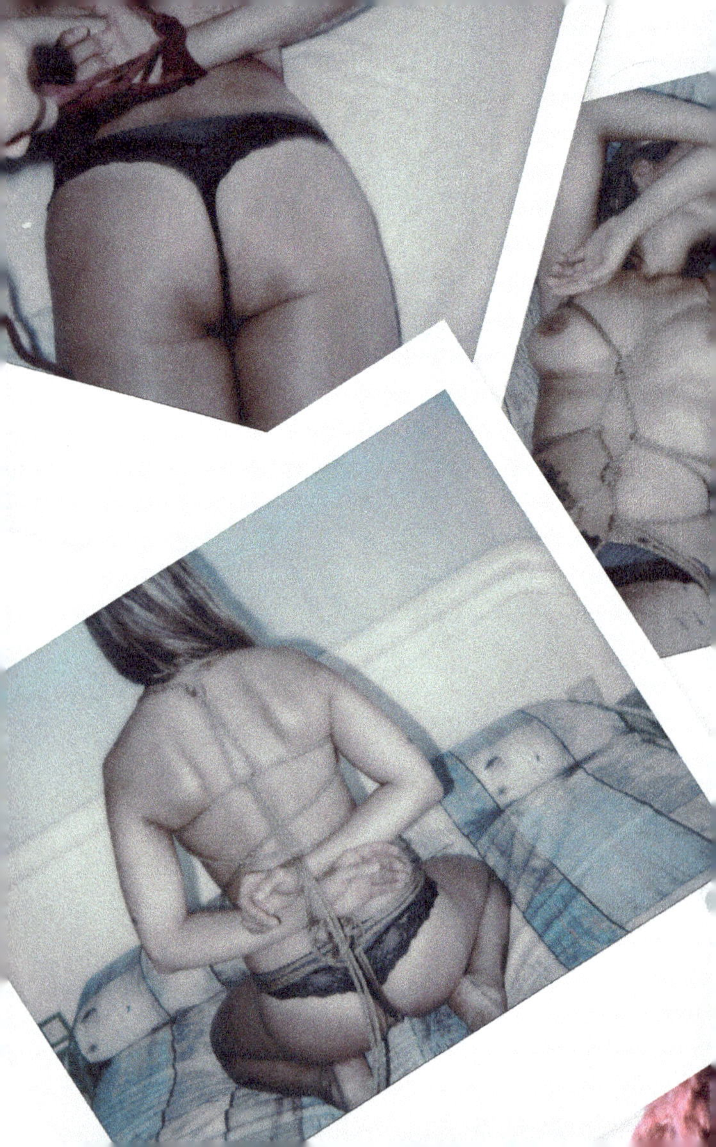

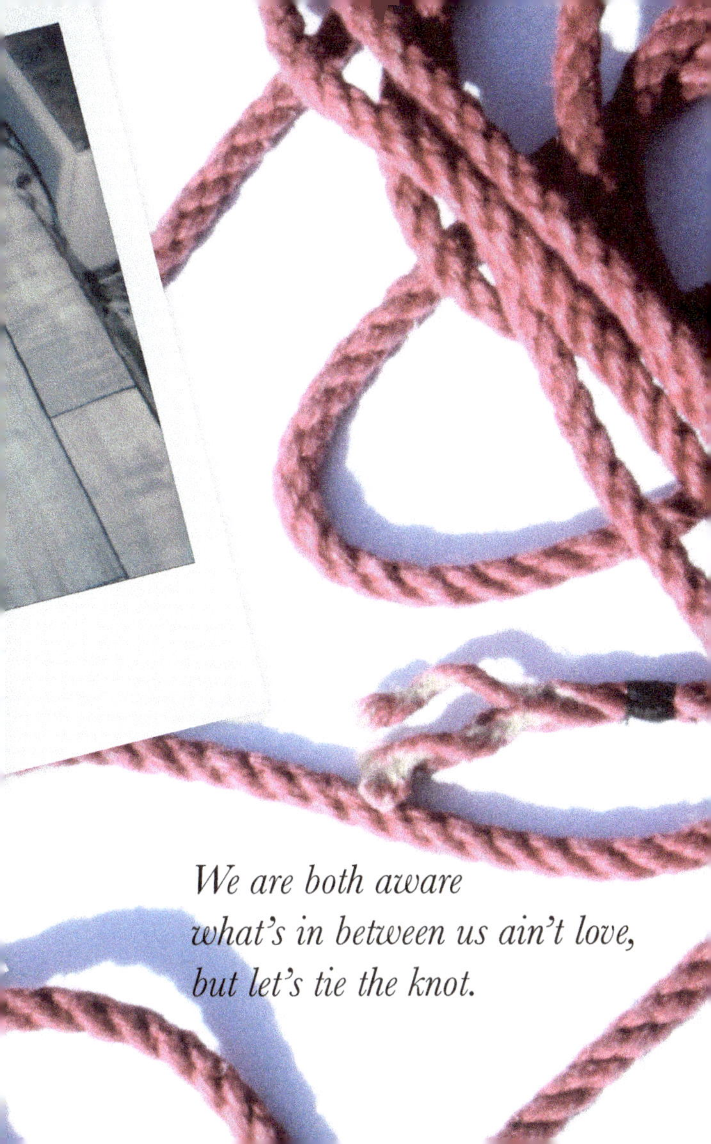
We are both aware
what's in between us ain't love,
but let's tie the knot.

*Depression is made
of lonely winter days and
trees with Christmas lights.*

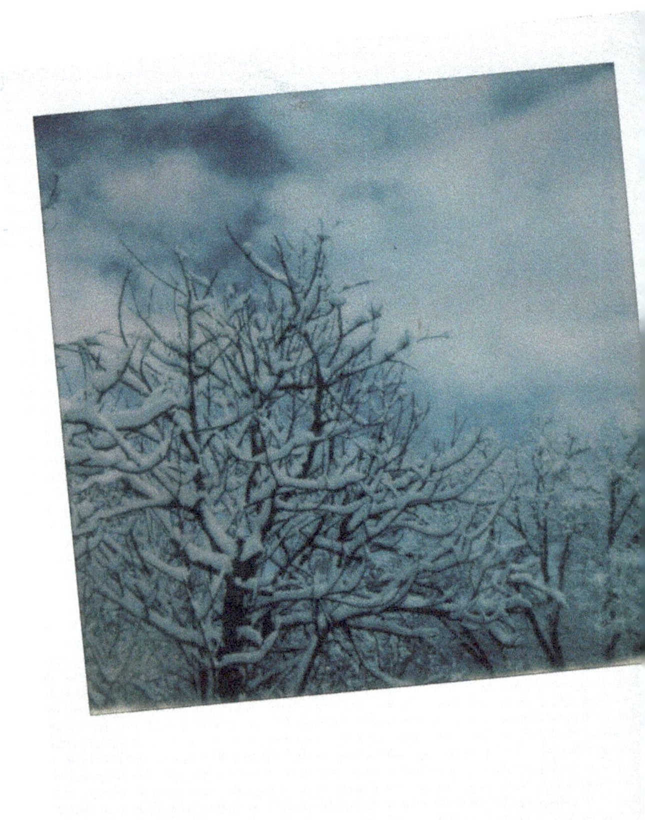

A white tree dances,
the snow falls in slow motion,
Winter is now here.

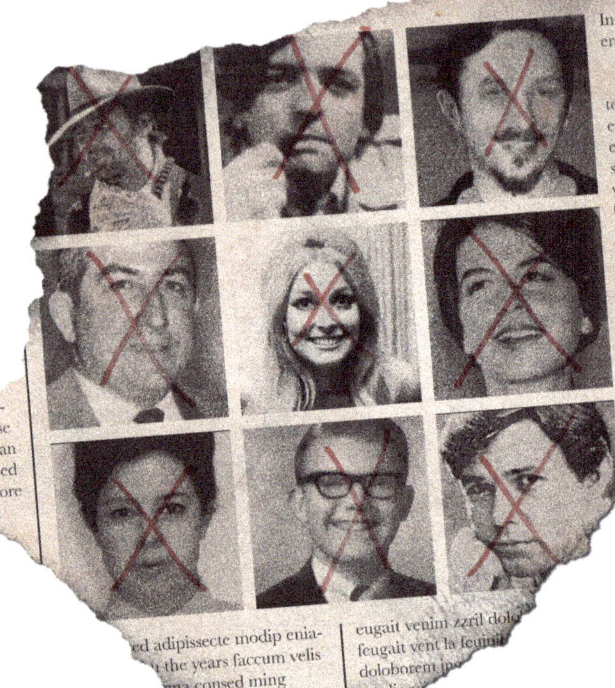

56

He lived all the years
that he took from his victims.
He died of old age.

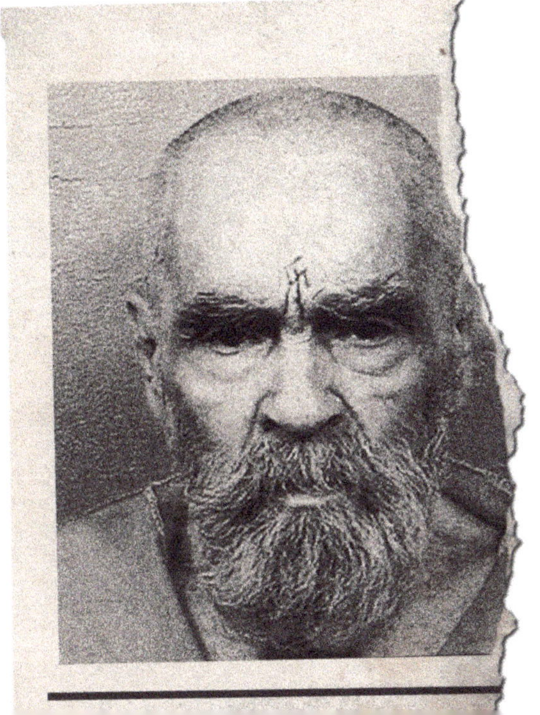

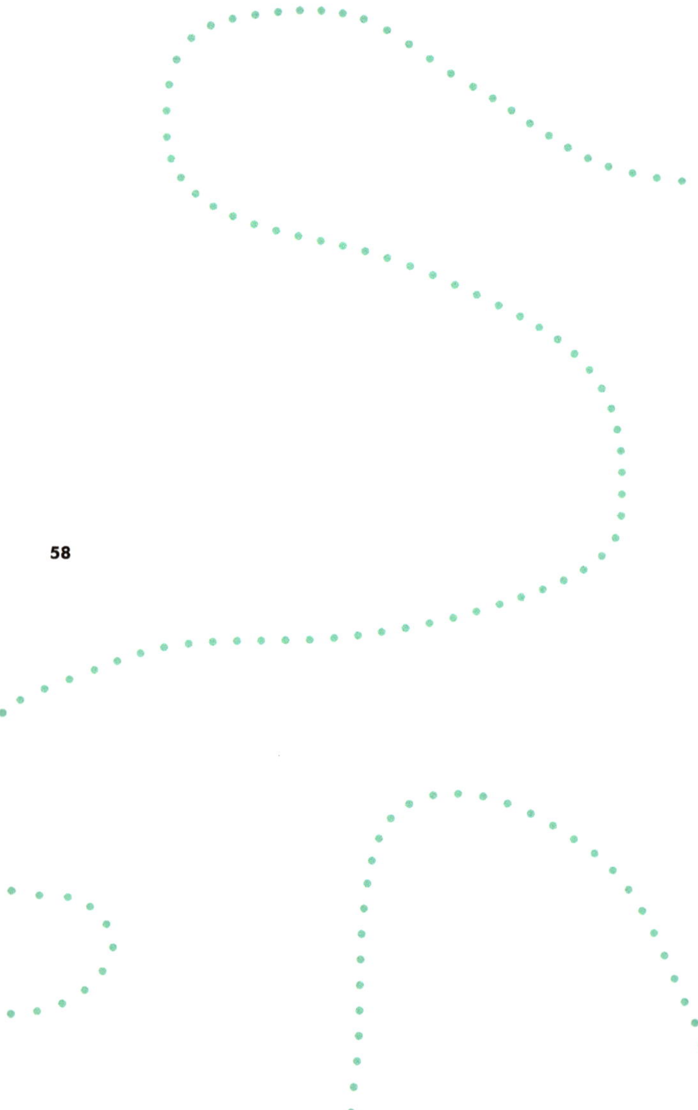

58

Exiled, kidnapped, sold, raped, adrift, and finally sent back home. Repeat.

Red lifesavers that
float on the sea, red tombstones
we choose not to see.

FASCISM RISING IS, PROBABLY, JUST A CASE OF PLANNED OBSOLESCENCE.

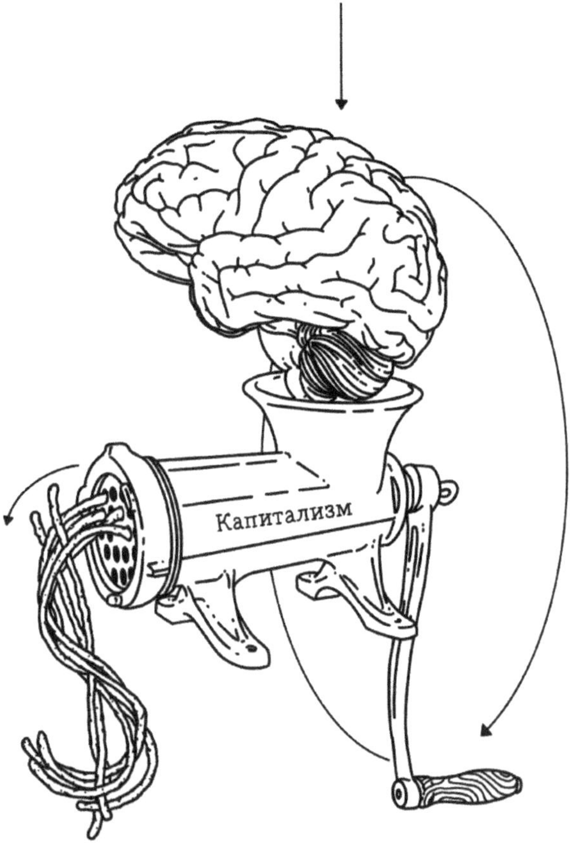

64

*Greed is a disease
and money is the virus,
too spread to be cured.*

There can't be justice
if gavels and guns are held
by the same two hands.

1789

Crimson guillotines,
golden thrones collecting dust,
blue blood bleeding red.

1799

Nothingness awaits
God is just men's ignorance
Darkness is relief.

*Pity us who stay
for we suffer your absence
when your light is gone.*

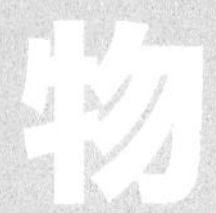
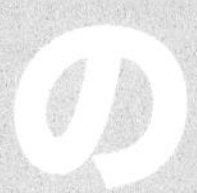

物の哀れ・ **Mono no aware.**

1.　(n) strong aesthetic sense; appreciation of the fleeting nature of beauty; pathos of things

CHAPTER 2

哀れ

I was happy, once.
It's tough when I remember 79
I was happy, once.

*My wounds won't heal, they
weep at the thought of you but
this price I can pay.*

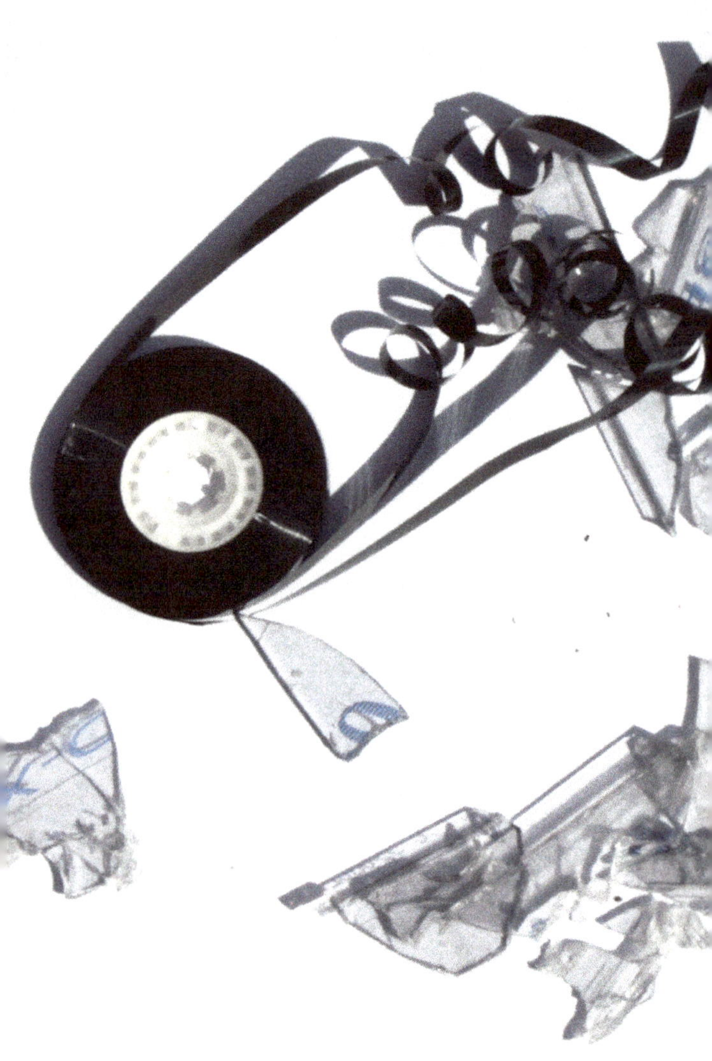

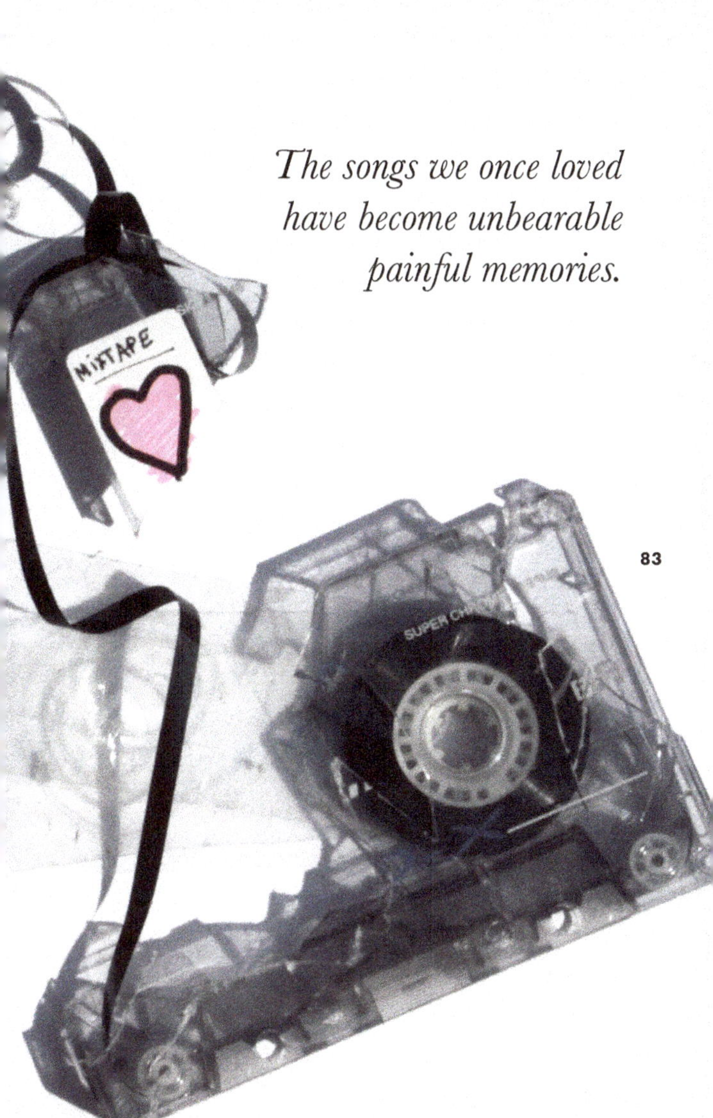
The songs we once loved
have become unbearable
painful memories.

MIXTAPE

*I shut myself in,
because in my head no one
hurts me but myself.*

Uncurable wound.
Love that keeps me from loving.
Self-inflicted pain.

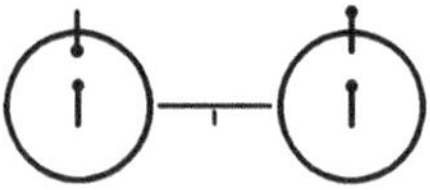

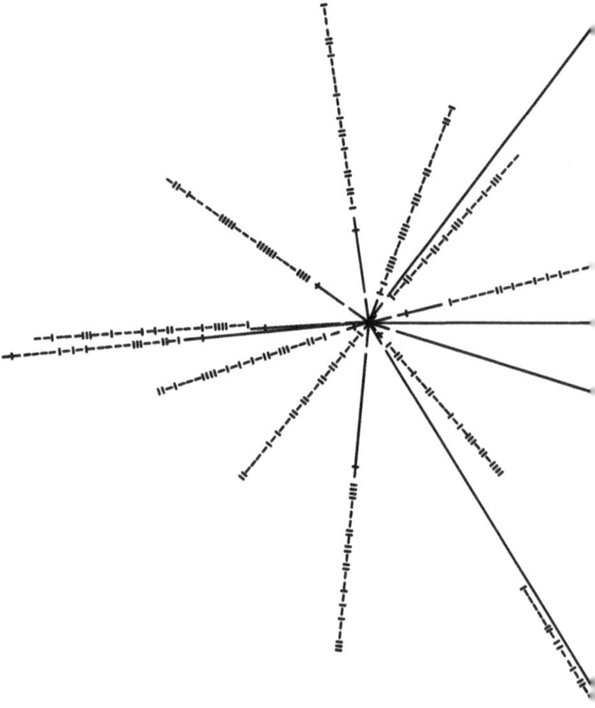

88

I look at the stars

*to remind myself of how
small everything is.*

I am a zombie
that slowly walks the earth, numb   91
and without purpose.

*Love that transcends time
and that transcends borders. Love
that transcends reason.*

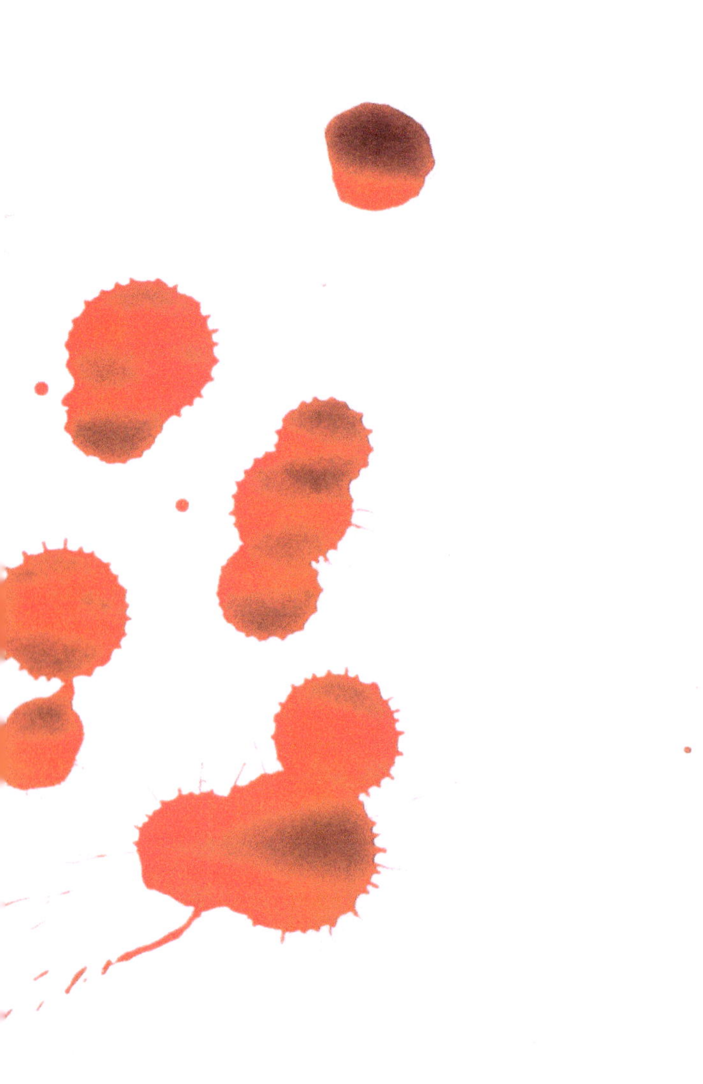

*Everyday is a
constant fight against the urge
to grab the razor.*

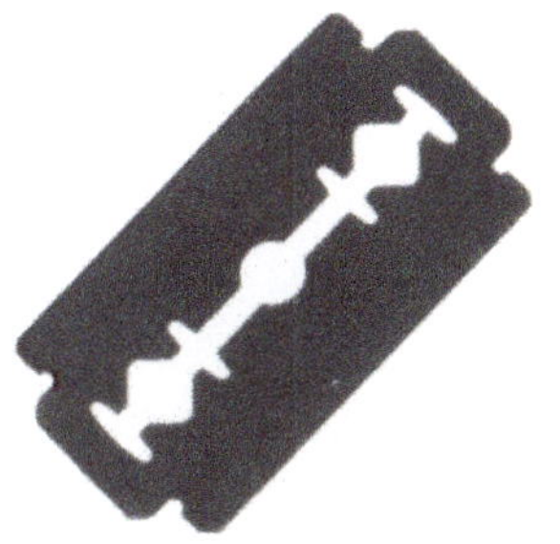

*I still have nightmamares,
and I don't mean in my sleep
but when I wake up.*

97

Where's the difference?
Dreams are real while they last.
Please, don't wake me up.

100

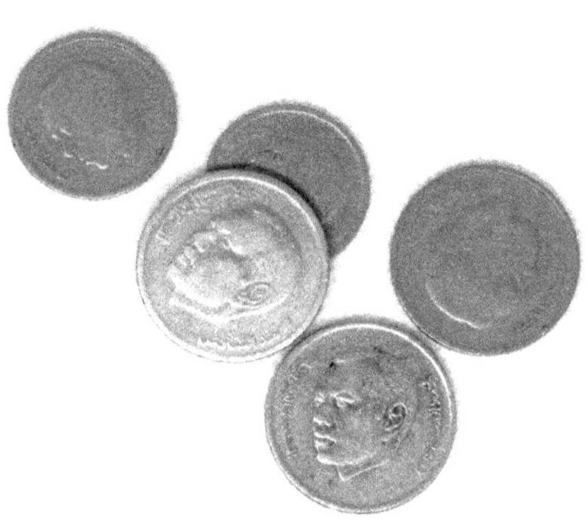

Maison de la Photographie
de Marrakech
1870 - 1950

40 dhs

Billet No 24977

Maison de la Photographie
46 Rue Ahal Fes — Marrakech
www.maisondelaphotographie.ma
maison@delaphotographiemarrakech@gmail.com
Tél : 05 24 38 57 21

I wrote "I'm Sorry"

at the back of a postcard

I never sent you.

*If the truth is that
you are only in my head,
I don't want to know.*

*She will find the one
and I'm scared it won't be me.
It scares me to death.*

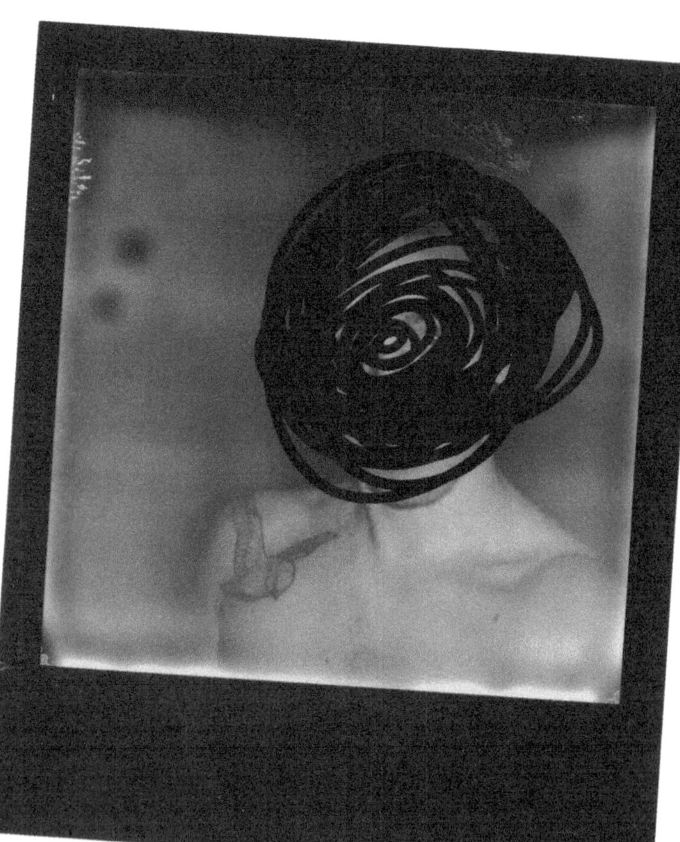

LOCKED IN, LIFE SENTENCE
IN A PRISON WITH NO BARS,
ONLY GREY MATTER.

108

*Don't kiss me in my
dreams unless you're there to kiss
me when I wake up.*

110

Too sad too often.
Like a snake in its prey's cave,
dreadful thoughts crawl in.

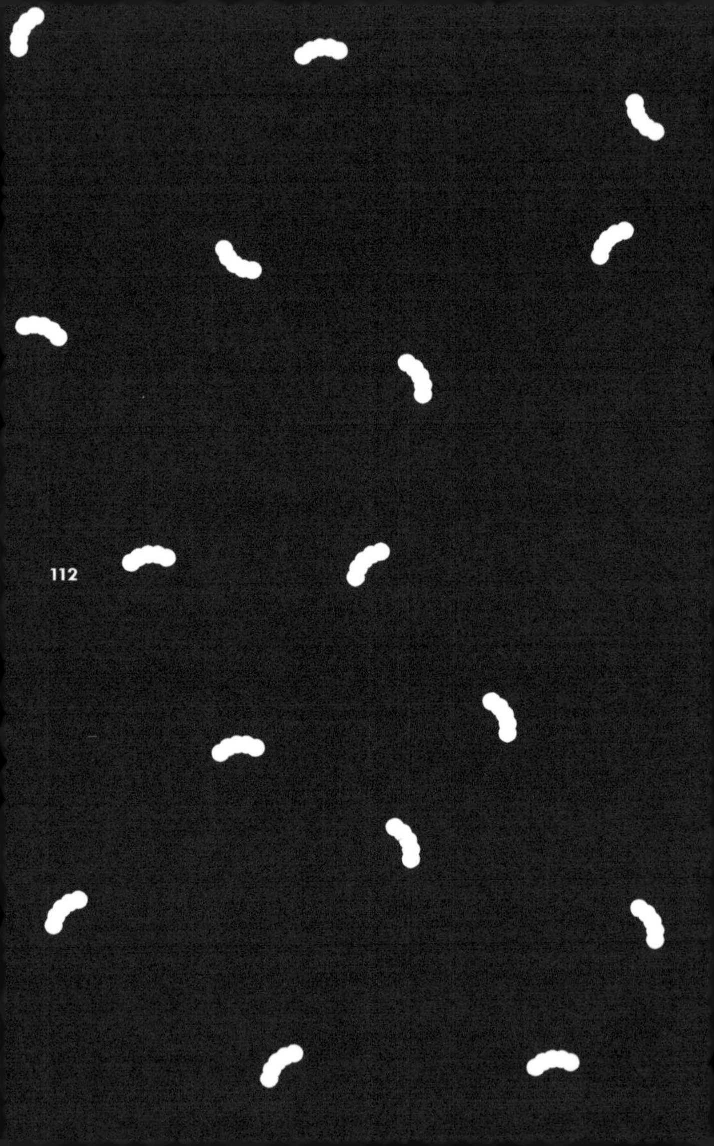

*Maybe my purpose
is simply to become a
feast for the maggots.*

I like her blue eyes
and her freckles, but I fell
in love with her mind.

EPILOGUE

*I wrote these for me,
because it was not healthy
to hold them inside.*

FEEDBACK

Did you love this book? Did you hate it? Would you like to discuss some of these poems with the author, talk about a poem you didn't comprehend because of its cryptic nature, or simply leave constructive criticism? You can do so via twitter: **@clashbooks**

ABOUT THE AUTHOR

Joel Amat Güell (born Joel Amat Güell) is not an academy award winning writer, he just draws things "for a a living". He has designed t-shirts and posters for companies and brands you've probably never heard of and for some others that you probably have.

JoelAmatGuell.com
Ig: @joelamatguell

ALSO BY CLASH BOOKS

* 9 7 8 1 9 4 4 8 6 6 4 7 1 *